GREAT BRITAIN & IRELAND'S

TOUGHEST GOLF HOLES

TOM HEPBURN

SELWYN JACOBSON

Salem House Publishers
Topsfield, Massachusetts

*P.G.A. Health Warning

Golfing *can* affect your health. If you are thin-skinned, weak-kneed, lilly-livered or suffer from congenital high handicapping, the Publishers and Authors join with the P.G.A. in urging you, before venturing onto any of our illustrated holes, to visit your Professional. And, if you've any sense, your doctor, your ski-instructor and the Man from the Prudential.

If you do insist on aiming for the record books (*you qualify just by completing the 18 holes — any score gets a mention*) the following tips may assist you in correct club choice, keeping your score down and getting back alive.

**Posthumous Golfers Anonymous*

SOME USEFUL DEFINITIONS

The Uphill Lie

McBaffie, in his "*Not On The Level*" (93rd edit.) insists the legs be well spread and the club gripped an inch further down the shaft to guarantee accuracy.

Casual Water

Golfers scorn taking the penalty drop from water, when all that's needed is a little application and a firm grip.

The Elements

Inclement weather *never* means an abandoned match. Perhaps an extra sweater, certainly a flask of Laphroaig.

Disclaimer
The publishers wish to take the opportunity to assure readers that none among them, keen golfers to a man though they may be, have at any time played any of the great golf holes herein illustrated. Neither, they wish to add, has anyone they have ever met played any of the holes and lived to tell about it. They therefore hereby decline any and all responsibility to such persons who, in playing any of these holes, finish with a double bogey, a ruined set of clubs or loss of life.

Cover photograph
They often do things differently in Welsh Wales: this upside down drop shot is no exception. Best to hit the green in one — or Dai trying.

Concept:
Tom Hepburn and Selwyn Jacobson
Text: Tom Hepburn
Artwork: John Cole, Tom Folwell
Photographs from: Barnaby's Picture,
Library British Tourist Authority, Picturepoint Ltd.
Printed in Hong Kong through Colorcraft Ltd

First published in the United States
by Salem House Publishers, 1989,
462 Boston Street, Topsfield Massachusetts, 01983

© Copyright 1983 Tom Hepburn and Selwyn Jacobson
ISBN 0 88162 358 8

All rights reserved. No part of this publication may be reproduced, stored in a retrieval system or transmitted in any form or by any means, electronic, mechanical, photocopying, recording, or otherwise, without the prior written permission of the publishers.

TRANSPORT & BASIC EQUIPMENT

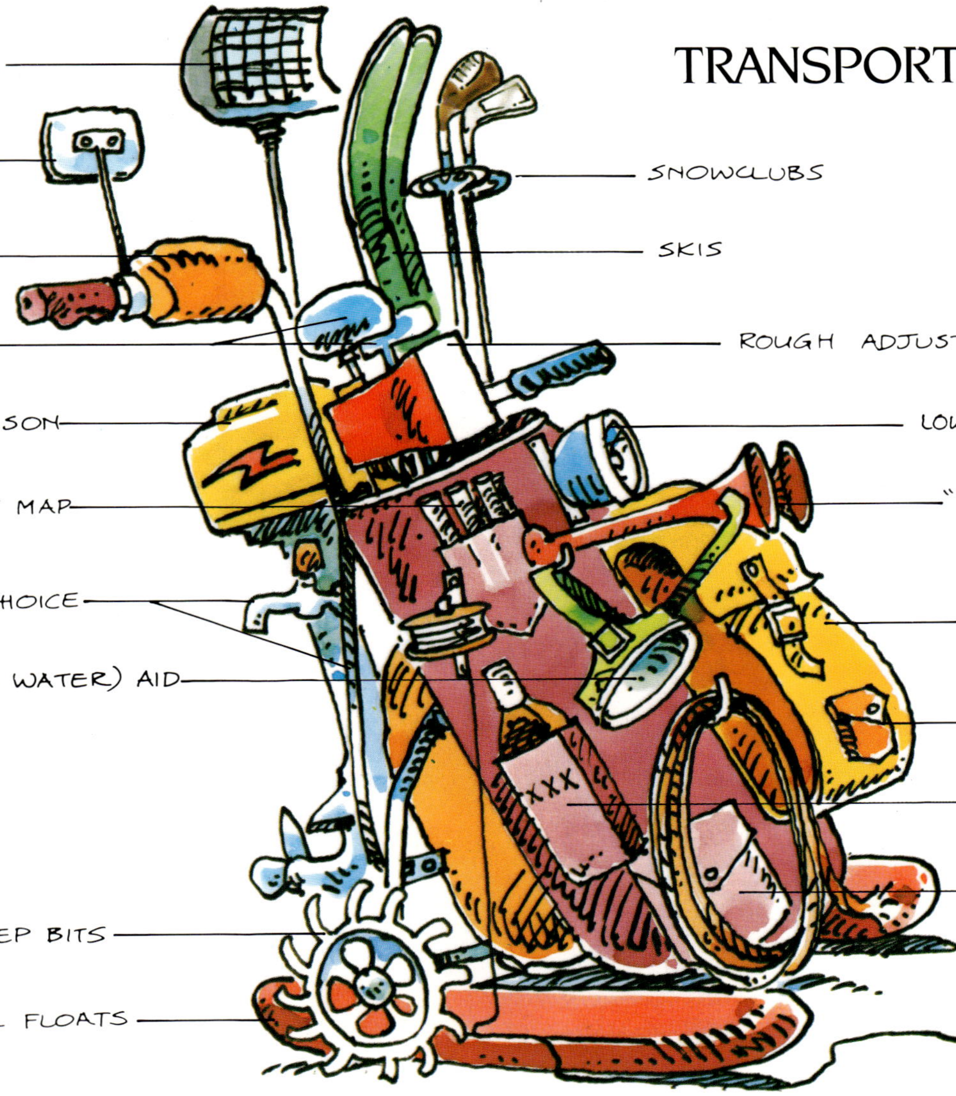

- RADAR
- VANITY & REVERSING MIRROR
- DISTRESS FLARE
- A FEW CLUBS (IN CASE BALL PLAYABLE)
- 270 H.P. JOHNSON
- ORDNANCE SURVEY MAP
- TUBULAR FRAME (& TAP) FILLED WITH BEVERAGE OF CHOICE
- HEAVY RAIN (OR CASUAL WATER) AID
- SPECIAL WHEEL RIMS FOR TRACTION ON STEEP BITS
- SNOW AND/OR WATER FLOATS
- SNOWCLUBS
- SKIS
- ROUGH ADJUSTER
- LOW CLOUD LAMP
- "FORE" KLAXONS
- 3 DAYS SURVIVAL RATIONS
- SPARE GOLF BALL (FOR WHEN STRING BREAKS)
- 12 YEAR OLD MALT
- SPARE POCKET FOR EMERGENCIES
- THE McBAFFIE "NEVER LOSE" BALL KIT WITH 6500 YARDS TWINE

THE ENEMY

Ordinary Birdie — Eagle — Albatross

THE AMMUNITION

Small British — Large American

SELECTED WEAPONS

1. **Baffie:** long approaches; sheltering behind during storms; emergency firewood supply.
2. **Spoon:** shallow (less than 1.8 fathoms) casual water; scoop shots from crevices; measuring Scotch into coffee.
3. **Cleek:** deep water recoveries — running noose catches ball, or with luck a fish.
4. **Niblick:** for taking divots on rocky surfaces; repelling wild animals; running amock with in mixed foursomes.

BEN NEVIS GOLF CLUB

McMONCK'S FOLLY
965 yards   par 5   1st hole

RAMBLING, even (at 14,280 yards off the Championship tees) lengthy by some standards, the 'South 18' here at Ben Nevis offers fine views and healthy exercise. As McBaffie's now out of print* classic "SCOTTISH COURSES — HOW TO DRINK THE 19TH'S" recommends "...*four hours out and three hours in, no guide necessary but good weather essential*". Though the clubhouse is hidden in the valley below, the 1st tee and green (foreground) and the 2nd and 9th greens are clearly visible. Visitors often come just to play this triangle, made famous by 'Bonnie Geordie' McMonck who was reputed to have driven a Model 'T' Ford along this route, playing every shot from the driver's seat. Unfortunately a broken axle near the 9th green caused his front wheels to encroach on the putting surface, and Geordie was set upon, with fatal results, by an irate Head Greenkeeper (long suspected of being a Jacobite sympathiser).

*(*A few copies still available from the author at 4s/6d each plus p.&p. 7¾d*)

BEN NEVIS GOLF CLUB

WHITECLIFFS COUNTRY CLUB

HOPING ARCH
325 yards   par 4   2nd hole

ATYPICAL busy day at one of Antrim's prettier seaside courses: our photograph (taken from Liam's Leap) shows two holes from what grows into an exasperating outward nine. Though our caption names the surprisingly hard-to-par 1st — the terrain is tricky and the gently sloping green does not favour the poorly executed approach — the spectacular 2nd is not the easy drop shot it seems. Many the distressed golfer, ball supply exhausted after trying in vain to land one on the putting surface, who has lurched ashen-faced back along the perilous pathway (seen just off the 1st fairway) to the splendid Clubhouse to renew his supply. This magnificent edifice, once Mad McGuire's milking shed, now boasts arguably the finest 19th in Northern Ireland and Head Barman Carlos McGillicuddy's quick sympathy and lightning-fast service often ensure that shaken golfers, rather than face a return to the 2nd tee, prefer to spend the rest of the day discussing what might have been.

WHITECLIFFS COUNTRY CLUB

SNOWDONIA GOLF & CLIMBING CLUB

THE DRIFTS
580 yards   par 5   3rd hole

THE difference between golfers and players has seldom been better underlined than in our photograph. There are some — mere players — who dash for the clubhouse at the first looming of a cloud; others — golfers to a man — quietly ignore climatic vagaries and play steadily on. To such sporting stalwarts a few feet of snow poses no problems, and when the keenly awaited new volume from J. Braid McBaffie *"The Snow Wedge — Play Winning Shots From Drifts"* is finally released, snow golfing is expected to become the in thing. One small word of warning though — never shout "Fore!" during the avalanche season without first a careful glance above. On this very course the late Club Captain and three colleagues failed to progress farther than the short 16th (**"PRECIPICE"**) during the admittedly harsh winter of '93. Visitors' attention is often drawn to the discreet plaque in the 19th commemorating the foursome's untimely disappearance.

SNOWDONIA GOLF & CLIMBING CLUB

CALLANISH COUNTRY CLUB

BUCHAN'S BUNKER
355 yards   par 3   4th hole

OVER the years students of John Buchan's novels and golf historians alike would often find their paths crossing here at Callanish. However it was not until the final stages of the Breastclete and Garynahine Longest Drive Into Loch Roag competition of '58 that the reason became clear. Searching desperately for useful hints to help preserve his unbeaten record, in that fine standard work "*McBAFFIE ON CASUAL WATER — HOW MUCH TO PUT IN YOUR MALT*", Hector McPustule came upon an undated letter signed by Buchan himself, explaining all. It seems Buchan, in the district researching locations for a new novel, had taken a well-earned break and accepted an invitation to play the new course. Casually told here on the tee to the short 4th that the entire course was laid out over 39 gigantic gravestones, Buchan seemingly became agitated and refused to play on. Instead he sat down in the bunker of this toughish par 3 and began scribbling furiously. It was not long before the world thrilled to his best seller "*THE THIRTY-NINE STEPS*". (Incidentally, McPustule lost the long drive competition that year — the string broke and he was disqualified for losing his ball.

CALLANISH COUNTRY CLUB

COLERAINE & DISTRICT GOLF CLUB

GIANT'S FAIRWAY
605 yards   par 5   5th hole

THIS deceptively tricky hole has been the undoing of many a promising round, yet seldom can any golfers have been so cheerfully tolerant of their bad luck as Ephraim and Thaddeus Paisley, who came simultaneously and spectacularly to grief here during the first round of the **Ballycastle and Milligan Point Licensed Victuallers Annual Fifty Best Customers Tournament.** Sensibly fortifying themselves en route from judiciously placed kegs of draught Guinness (with best wishes from your Sponsors), the Paisley twins (no relation) arrived mellow if unsteady at the 5th tee. Ephraim, who'd never been properly re-connected to his left foot (a legacy from The Troubles) failed to cope with the awkwardly contoured fairway and ere long found himself firmly wedged in a cleft. Always the gentleman, Thaddeus hastened to his aid but alas in trying to prise Ephraim free with his putter, he too became inextricably stuck. Working on the theory that if they could just relax enough they'd slide free, the lads proceeded to relax as much as they could. In an impromptu after dinner speech that evening, Thaddeus thanked the Sponsors, whose continued supply of relaxing fluids had contributed so successfully to their final release.

COLERAINE & DISTRICT GOLF CLUB

YESNABY CASTLE MUNICIPAL LINKS

MODRED'S LOT
210 yards   par 3   6th hole

IN the true Dark Ages, during those years which followed the infamous Royal edict against "The Playing of the Gowf", when the King's men ranged far and wide apprehending anyone who spoke too loosely in taverns of how they played the long 15th last weekend, there crept into our language those dread words "Bogey-men", or "The beating of the Bogey". But even then, far to the north, a tiny band of low-handicap dissidents stood firm against the Crown, the treacherous waters of the Pentland Firth a buffer of safety. Orcadian nights being as long as they are, a nucleus of Twilight Golfers grew around the fine natural links at Yesnaby. Leader of this brave band was none other than the legendary Modred Bews who, when in form, would take his favourite cleek here at the 6th, then using his famous cable-throwing prowess hurl clubs, bag and trundler across the gap onto the green, dive down into the seething cauldron below, swim over, climb up and, to the rapturous cheers of his regular gallery, putt out — often for a birdie. This hole is in fact named in posthumous honour of Modred's final, unsuccessful dive, taken at low tide during the final round of the Stronsay Open of '45.

YESNABY CASTLE MUNICIPAL LINKS

CARRICK-A-REDE MUNICIPAL GOLF CLUB

CLIFFHANGER

380 yards   par 4   7th hole

CAN there be a golfer who hasn't experienced, at least once in his life, that dread feeling of combined frustration, deflation and utter dejection when, on turning up fit and eager on a crisp clear morning to meet three friends on the 1st tee, he finds (1) it is Ladies Day; (2) a neighbouring Club has been invited over for a Stableford; (3) they have already teed off on the 1st, 6th and 9th; (4) vast numbers are still milling about near the Secretary's office; (5) quite a few of the larger ones are directing suspicious and antagonistic looks at the male interlopers, and (6) one or two are even moving in their direction, putters raised threateningly? Perhaps redressing the balance a little, our photograph taken on Carrick's pretty links shows the unmistakable figure of Clodagh Fishbaum, vivacious wife of the Club Captain — a study in restrained (*will the buggers never clear the green?*) ire — out for a practice round and stuck behind a couple of slow moving groups.

CARRICK-A-REDE MUNICIPAL GOLF COURSE

ABERSTRUMBLE COUNTRY CLUB

THE DIP
145 yards   par 3   8th hole

RECORD books are rewritten rather often around the Pembroke way, mostly because of the exciting challenge of clever green placements, but not least because of Blodwyn Herewini the New Zealand Amateur Sheep-Dipping Champion whose rampaging demonstration tour round Wales has kept 19th's buzzing for years. Blodwyn (named after her grandmother, a keen Lions supporter) because of giant biceps built up from years of hurling sheep around, could hit a golf ball further than most men. Yet her greatest triumph came at this short par 3 at Alberstrumble when she birdied the hole twice the same day — and this remember was before the bridge was built! Success alas went to her head and she celebrated by hurling the members of her foursome and five spectators off the green before she could be restrained. Her defiant cry of 'Valbesan, Valbesan!' as she was led handcuffed back to the Clubhouse was interpreted as a Maori warcry.

(Blodwyn of course went on to even greater triumphs. Her autobiography, "BIG DIPPER" is expected next year.)

ABERSTRUMBLE COUNTRY CLUB

RHAEDR FAWR GOLF CLUB

ABERA-ATION
368 yards par 4 9th hole

THERE'S something about a waterfall guaranteed to bring out the devil in any course architect. Alonso Daffyd Podmarsh II was no exception and his original green placement (circa 1873) here on the otherwise attractive 9th brought many a tear to the eye of even the most hardened of golfers. However, later that decade — long before golf balls were so advertised by their makers not only to fly farther but to withstand the ravages of hook, slice and shank — and when the merest Scotch Mist floating in from over the border turned stream into torrent and played very havoc with the best of approaches, Alonso returned as Guest Celebrity to partner Welsh golf extremist Gwilliam 'Dai the Divot' Gwilliams in the Llandyfrdog and Llanerhymedd Pro-Am, only to find the green completely submerged. Using his Travelling Pro's Kit, it was the work of a moment for Al to tunnel under the green, construct the natty retaining wall still seen today, drive the green and putt out for a birdie. To this day Rhaeadr Fawr remains one of the most attractive golf holes worth playing well in Anglesey.

RHAEDR FAWR GOLF CLUB

SKYE GOLF & BOATING CLUB

NETTIE'S NEEDLE
160 yards   par 3   10th hole

SHOULD the casual visitor to the Isle of Skye, lured these days more by the promise of exciting golf than by the prospect of a tramp in the Cuillins, hear in the clear and crystal air the sound of a distant high handicapper singing the Club Song... "♫♪ *Speed bonny ba' like a bird on the wing* ..♫♪" he can be fairly sure the notes are floating down the glen from "Nettie's Needle", scene of a near-tragedy during the Ladies Pairs in '92. That desperate day Bathsheba McMurtrie, cup-holder and hot favourite, was partnered by Anastasia 'Fat Nettie' Rintoul, a lady whose immense girth had been even further widened by participation the evening before (successfully) in the Portree Pork Pie Eating competition. Nettie became firmly wedged in the tunnel — in those days a mere 4' wide — leading to the 10th tee. Determined not to let her partner down, the fat one decided to drive from where she stuck. Alas her ball riccoched off the rocky wall to embed itself in a roll of fat so delicately placed that it quite ruined her short game, and the pair had to concede.

(Note: the improved 18th tee to the long (1082 yard) last hole can be seen in our photograph, with the clubhouse in the background).

SKYE GOLF & BOATING CLUB

TINTAGEL GOLF & COUNTRY CLUB

PENDRAGON'S PERIL
480 yards   par 4   11th hole

THIS placid scene scarcely hints at the torrid sporting events of yesteryear. The poet Tennyson, himself a low handicapper, made certain of Tintagel's place in history in his 'Morte d'Arthur', the famous English Pro's saga now the accepted authority on the Open Championships of the Dark to Middle Ages — formative years in British golf! Alf was a stickler for his rule book (every Club has one) and after a few meads in the 19th was wont to ramble on a bit about the old days when the Club was still known as Lyonesse Links. His favourite anecdote was of the big grudge match between Modred Bews and Alastair Le Fey from Orkney and local heros Arthur Pendragon, Lyonesse Club Captain at the time, playing with T.B.S. Bedivere (+2). 'Arthur's Army' as Big Arthur's supporters were called, were out in force but alas Bedivere, having shanked badly into a mere, foolishly asked advice 'from someone not his caddy...'

"Ah, my Lord Arthur, whither shall I go?
Where shall I hide my forehead and my eyes?"

Of course he was immediately disqualified, and in a blind rage grabbed Arthur's cleek and hurled it into a nearby lake; caddy Sam White, rightly plunging in to retrieve the club (they floated in those days) alas caught his legs in underwater weed and was last seen waving the club wildly above his head before disappearing forever beneath the waves. Dispirited, neither Arthur nor Bedivere played again.

TINTAGEL GOLF & COUNTRY CLUB

HAG'S HEAD COUNTRY CLUB

NO MOHER

490 yards   par 4   12th hole

WHEN TRAINEE caddy old Ezekiel Moher farted in front of Sir Aloysius O'Brien's horse (the O'Briens always rode to golf) that incredibly hot summer day in '77, little did he realise his tone poem in (accidentally) F-flat would lead to the improvement of perhaps the finest seaside course in the west coast of Ireland. Not surprisingly the mare, a fastidious creature, stepped backwards in some alarm; and as this event took place on the precarious ledge which forms the 12th tee (the green is dog-legged north round the mist-enshrouded cliff) the resultant fatality was never in doubt. When the reading of Sir Aloysius' will confirmed his love of the game by providing for the construction of the final six holes, grateful members erected a tower nearby in his memory and renamed the Club in honour of his wife (long accepted as the ugliest woman in County Clare). Old Zeke, in atonement, never again played past the 12th hole. Instead he would deliberately chip a commemorative (practice) ball into the sea near where Sir Aloysius disappeared, then trudge sadly back to the clubhouse for a recuperative pint.

HAG'S HEAD COUNTRY CLUB

LAKELAND LINKS GOLF CLUB

N E E D L E D

205 yards — par 3 — 13th hole

MUCH has been written about the influence exerted on those of the poetic persuasion by the grandeur and tranquility of the English Lake District. Less well known perhaps is that more than one such man of letters suffered from quite a different type of addiction; though never on less than a 24, scarce a day passed, rain or shine, which failed to see young Willie Wordsworth out on the Links thrashing away at his fairway woods. That he took his game seriously was never in doubt — witness the day he turned up for a friendly nine holes with his neighbour 'Slammin Sammy' Coleridge (a 22-handicapper who when under the influence would claim he once, in a foursome with three intoxicated wedding guests, scored an albatross!) only to find his Club were holding their Mixed Foursomes qualifying round. His day ruined, Willie wrote savagely of the scene in the following month's issue of the Club newsletter...

Into the Lake, behind the trees
Fluffing and duffing into the breeze
Ten thousand saw I at a glance
Lifting their heads, with rotten stance.

There was of course a call for Willie's resignation, but he talked his way out of it by claiming he'd been writing about — of all unlikely things — daffodils!

LAKELAND LINKS GOLF CLUB

LAND'S END GOLF CLUB

BAD TIDE-INGS
290 yards   par 4   14th hole

AMADEUS
Treverithick, in his privately printed
monograph "THE PASTIE —
CORNWALL'S ANSWER TO THE BAFFIE?" dwelt
— and few would argue the point — at considerable
length on the need to master recovery shots from tricky rocky
lies. Thirty five years as assistant Ladies Coach ensured Amadeus
knew how to get off his rocks but even he couldn't cope with the
calamitous conditions surrounding the Club Champs that winter of
'42 when frenzied seas hurled themselves against a 14th hole which
even on the balmiest of days was described locally as making the
18th at Pebble Beach look like a backyard putting green. Time and
— particularly in this case — tide wait for no golfer, something
Amadeus, last away in the final round and four strokes in the lead,
forgot that wild afternoon. He just made it over the swing bridge
(seen in our photograph here at low tide) and had played a
safe iron across to the right for the preferred approach.
Alas while breasting the turgid seas back over, a surging
wave twitched his favourite niblick from a numbed
hand. Uttering a mad cry Amadeus plunged in
after it and was swept far out to sea,
conceding the match, the club and his life,
in that order.

LAND'S END GOLF CLUB

SNOWDON MUNICIPAL GOLF CLUB

OLD PUFFER

805 yards   par 5   15th hole

THOUGH it ought not to be, and indeed seldom is, confused with the nearby select private club (see our 3rd hole), this fine public course nevertheless boasts some intriguing golfing tests. Originally the Llanberis Llinks, the then nine hole layout was renamed (though mis-spelled) in '37 in honour of local-boy-made-good Philip Snowden, whose promising amateur golfing career was severely curtailed by his unfortunate bicycle accident. It is believed a borrowed baffie caught in his front spokes as he pedalled down from the clubhouse to the 1st tee, seen middle left in our photograph. He was tipped a good 7-iron down the slope but went on to fulfil his destiny in an even more dangerous game, in which he progressed to Chancellor of the Exchequer. Here on the long 15th big hitters often play across the valley, hoping for a safe lie to reach the green in two; lesser mortals normally plump for a 5-wood across-right to the railway line which, as it so often does in British courses, runs by the fairway, and so progress in easy stages up towards the Clubhouse. Elderly members have been known to wait several days for the next train up to conserve valuable energy.

SNOWDON MUNICIPAL GOLF CLUB

FOXHOUSE GOLF CLUB

HOLE-IN-THE-TOAD
180 yards   par 3   16th hole

ANECDOTES abound in England's more northern 19th's ad nearly nauseam of golfers claiming to have played record rounds with various quantities of ferrets stuffed down their plus-fours. But details such as angle of incisors, nose-to-bum length, viciousness per inch^3, pale into insignificance when *Hardcastle's Giant Toad* is mentioned. The famous Brigham Hardcastle's two sons were responsible for this obscure Derbyshire legend, Reg one slippery evening at the Drunken Duck betting his brother Parsifal he could give him three strokes *and* play with a toad down his trousers. Parsifal agreed on condition he supplied the beastie, and on the morning of the match produced such a toad as England had never seen, the result of some hasty cross-breeding with a Yorkshire Terrier. Aghast but game, Reg fought through to the 16th where, somehow, the toad gained control. Exactly what happened next is uncertain, but it is locally believed that the curious shape of the rock which forms the 16th green had much to do with the behaviour of the toad which, after eating Reg, escaped into the moors where it bred like (and probably with) a rabbit. Perhaps one reason why it is now a regular and popular item on the menu of Foxhouse G.C.'s fine dining rooms!

FOXHOUSE GOLF CLUB

CLUB NAME WITHELD — SEE BELOW

McBAFFIE'S BANE
365 yards   par 4   17th hole

INITIALLY purloined by, and later most fortuitously recovered from the kleptomaniacal arsonist Gaylord Peebles IV from the charred remains of the J. Braid McBaffie Golf Memorabilia Museum's west wing during the big blaze of '32, this photograph deserves pride of place on any golfer's wall. Seen addressing his drive into a typical Scottish water hazard is none other than H. Vardon McBaffie, 7th son of the celebrated course architect and to this day a figure of wild surmise in *****shire, his disappearance at this very hole even now unexplained. McBaffie senior, himself a 7th son, believed his family had 'the sight' and swears he saw, as in a dream, young Vardon hitting a 400 yard drive towards a misty, perfect green where mini-kilted maidens sang softly. Lesser gifted mortals reckon Vardon fell into a deep pool while trying to rescue a duffed shot and, reluctant to relinquish his grip on a new mashie, sank to the bottom. Whichever, sympathetic to a great man's loss the Publishers have agreed to supress the name of this golf club — now approaching shrine status — and have considerately named the hole in honour of a very sad event.

CLUB NAME WITHELD — SEE ABOVE

STONEHENGE COUNTRY CLUB

SACRI LEDGE
412 yards   par 4   18th hole

MANY the printed dissertation on this, the most venerable of England's country clubs; how little though we have found out of its origins, shrouded as they are in the misty past of golf's very beginnings. Yet if it hadn't been for that curious coincidence at the '57 **Architect's Invitation Best Ball**, we'd be even more in the dark. The identification by A.J.M. McAretz (R.I.B.P.G.A.) of the now world-famous chalky white drawing on the stone which supports the 18th green as an early Neolithic baffie brought two elderly historians to blows. And when he followed this up next round with a badly topped drive which chipped away a fragment of stone at the base to reveal part of runic inscription, there was even a letter to the Times (unpublished owing to a union dispute). Roughly translated, the runes tell of an event known then as "The Archdruid's Chalice", and three times mentions the names Stan and Boadicea Hengist. That the standing stones were originally laid out as a tight little golf course, and that the event in question was obviously a mixed pairs tournament, is no longer a point of contention. But the suggestion that the course was named in honour of 3-times winner Stan Hengist is still arguable.

STONEHENGE COUNTRY CLUB

Salem House Publishers
Topsfield, Massachusetts